Words From the Heart

Heidy De La Cruz

Illustration by
Michelle Reynoso

Acknowledgment

First, I want to thank God for the gift of writing and blessing this process to be able to get my words out in the world. Secondly, I want to thank my loving husband, Jonathan, for believing in me and encouraging me during this process. And thirdly, I want to dedicate this book to my children, Lia and Jayden. You two keep me going every day. I love you.

Content

THE TRIALS

Dark Place

Sometimes when you're in a dark place

Scary uncontrollable thoughts come to mind....

It's not something you would normally think about or even come close to consider

But when you fall into the dark

The thoughts starts creeping in......like a repeating nightmare

The pain is deep, unbearable, sharp

Overwhelming and consuming

It takes your breath away

You try to scream but no one can hear you

Nothing comes out.

You reach out for help...no one is around

No one understands

You cannot explain the unexplainable

And it's always in the back of your mind

The dark place is just one slip away......

Thoughts

Who controls your thoughts......

Those dark thoughts

Deep thoughts

The ones you lose yourself

Lose yourself that the way out seems like a maze

A glaze

Who controls your thoughts......

The transparent ones

Thoughts you can't hide

The ones that drown you like a tide

A wave

Who controls your thoughts......

Happy ones

The feeling of being unstoppable

Unbreakable

A dream you're running to chase

The light that can't be tamed

Who controls your thoughts......

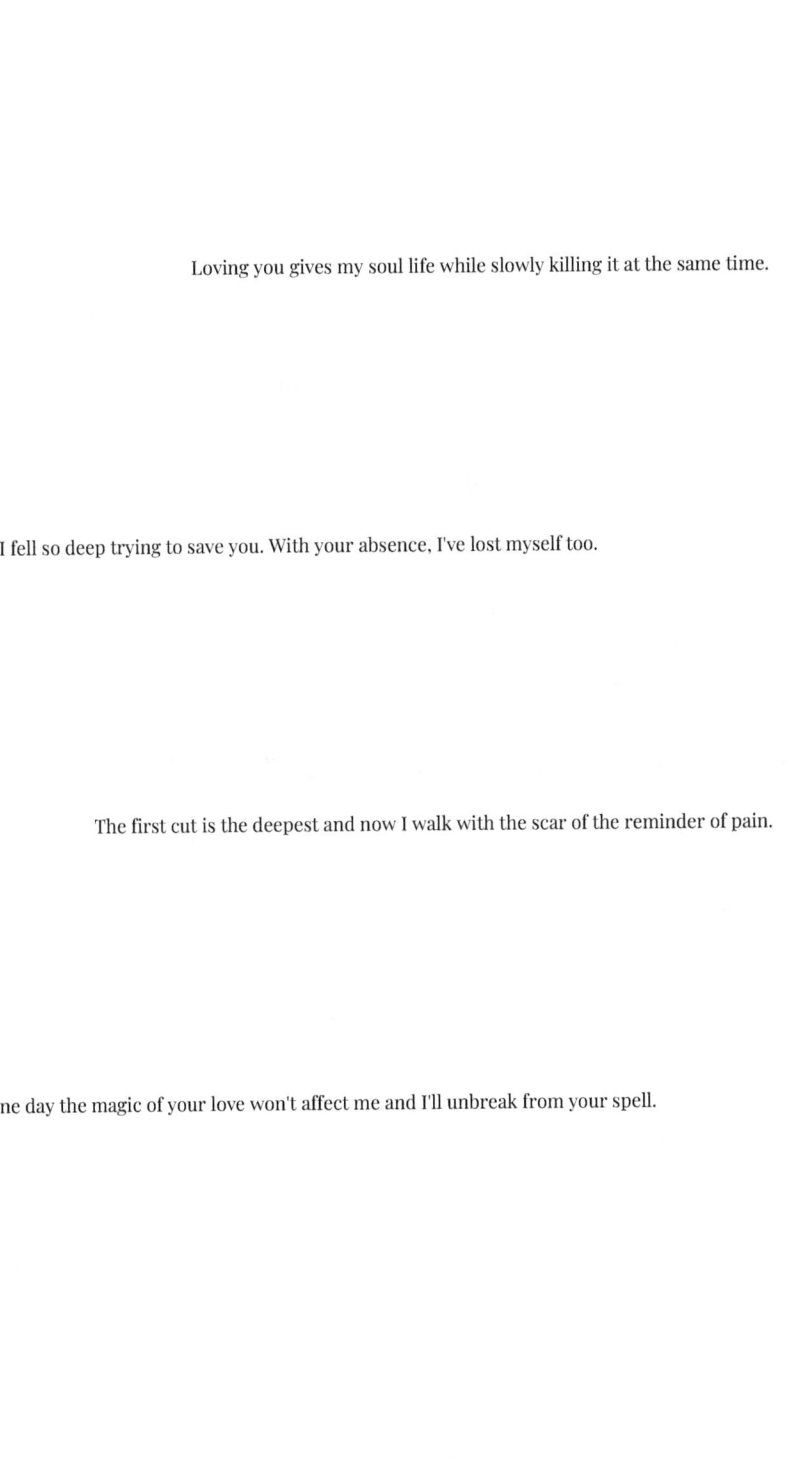

Loving you gives my soul life while slowly killing it at the same time.

I fell so deep trying to save you. With your absence, I've lost myself too.

The first cut is the deepest and now I walk with the scar of the reminder of pain.

One day the magic of your love won't affect me and I'll unbreak from your spell.

The sun is out but I can't feel its warmth.

The birds sing but I can't hear their chirp.

Roses blossom but I can't smell their
nectar.

People crack jokes but I miss the
punchline.

TV no longer an entertainment.

Reading is no longer an escape.

No more pleasure in what was
pleasurable before.

Exhaustion is the norm. Getting out of
bed is a hassle.

Sleep, all I want is to sleep.

Forever

No appetite

Just leave me alone.......to rot.

They say, "Just be happy"

If it were that easy I wouldn't choose to be
unhappy

Thoughts are uncontrolled.

Whispering, are you worthy? End
it all.

Pain, suffering, void feeling,
emptiness, loneliness.

No one understands.

To complete one task drains me.

Sucks my energy.....all of it.

Crying

Lots of crying.

For what? For nothing....for all.

Distance. I keep my distance.

Communication is disrupted.

Words don't even make sense.

Just like this poem.

I'm a mess.

Depression

I'm in search for the wand to undo the spell, the haze, all around me all I see is you. Break me free.

The feeling of drowning is nonstop, will I ever make it to the top?

Are You Living Your Truths?

If walls could talk would they tell my secrets or would they burn down with them when the match lights up in flames?

Some stories should never be told.

They might break your heart or make you be seen in a new pair of eyes.

Are you always living your truth or is the truth something you won't be able to handle?

The truth is layered deep, hidden like a mask. Only to be seen when I choose to show.

If the pillow could talk would it say whose all laid? Would it repeat all the conversations said on it?

Sometimes silence says more than a thousand words.

The silence tells the truth

Tells the story that shouldn't be told

Shouldn't be known

Lies protect while tearing apart deeply

But who protects your secrets?

Have you forgiven me yet

Have you forgiven me yet

For the lies told

For the mind games played

For the dreams sold

Have you forgiven me yet

For the mistreatment

The emotional abuse

The heartbreak

Have you forgiven me yet

For the loveless sex

Making you fall

The pretending

Have you forgiven me yet

I've already destroyed you. I've already broken you in a million pieces. I've ripped out your heart and stomped on it. You just don't know it yet.

I would speak but it was like a different language to you. I showed you how I needed to be loved. But you showed me hurt. You loved me in the most wicked way, but it's the only way you knew how. I just needed you to hold me, but you gave me absences instead. I thought this was love. How foolish.

Can't ever be happy for long. The devil catches up quick.

You were the teacher for loving, now be the teacher of forgetting.

Please understand my life was you, when you walked away you took everything with you.

Poison is what you feed

Air is what you speak

The key and knife you hold

Killing me softly with every lie told

Knowing you're not good for me why can't I walk away

We said goodbye in every possible way imaginable. But was it really a goodbye? & I do regret falling for you because now I have to live with the pain that you'll never be mine.

Have you ever loved someone so much that even though you cannot be together you still want them in your life? Somehow. Some way.

I kept running back to you. Back to the hurt, betrayal, and suffering. Thinking each time you would help me cure. Like a drug, I was an addict. The withdrawals were a monster. Finally my eyes were opened.

Let me know if you really loved me or if it was all a play so my heart can stop wishing you'd stay.

Rolling stones, my heart crumbles. As the pain crawls in. Air leaves my lungs but doesn't return. Suffocation at its finest. I forgot how to breathe.

Always on the edge playing with fire, but are you ready for when you get burned?

The clouds rumbling, the soul is sad. The tear falls with the raindrops. It doesn't rain forever. Will the smile come back?

It was exhausting loving for both of us. It was draining fighting for both of us. It was challenging caring for both of us. It wasn't worth falling apart for you.

How do I calm the battlefield in my head? Half the time believing I'm worth it & half the time thinking why am I even here?

There is power in your words, like a double edge sword, giving me life while killing me at the same time.

As time goes by, I hope somehow, some way, you keep my memory alive.

You hit me as you smashed into me, over and over again. Pulled me back and down again. Took over my body as if I was your slave. Made me feel dirty, low. Left your mark on my body visible for the next two weeks. You think that's sex? The pleasure was only for you.

Through the distance, I waited....through the hardship I stayed...I dreamt of the day of your arrival time and time again....counted down the days of when space was no longer between us....all while holding it down....fantasizing about how things would be.....but reality hit hard real quick....it all looked nice in my head....was sleeping on clouds and dreamland....it quickly became a nightmare....one I can't forget.

Even a glimpse of my mind would terrify you.

The voices in my head accompany me during your absence in the night. The nightmares hold me and fears cradle me.

I need you to be strong, I need you to be firm, I need you to not answer the phone every time I call asking for more.

It's sad to think about what it could have been.

I counted the days, hours, & seconds to be with you now I made a home in other arms.

You cut my wings so I had to learn to fly without them.

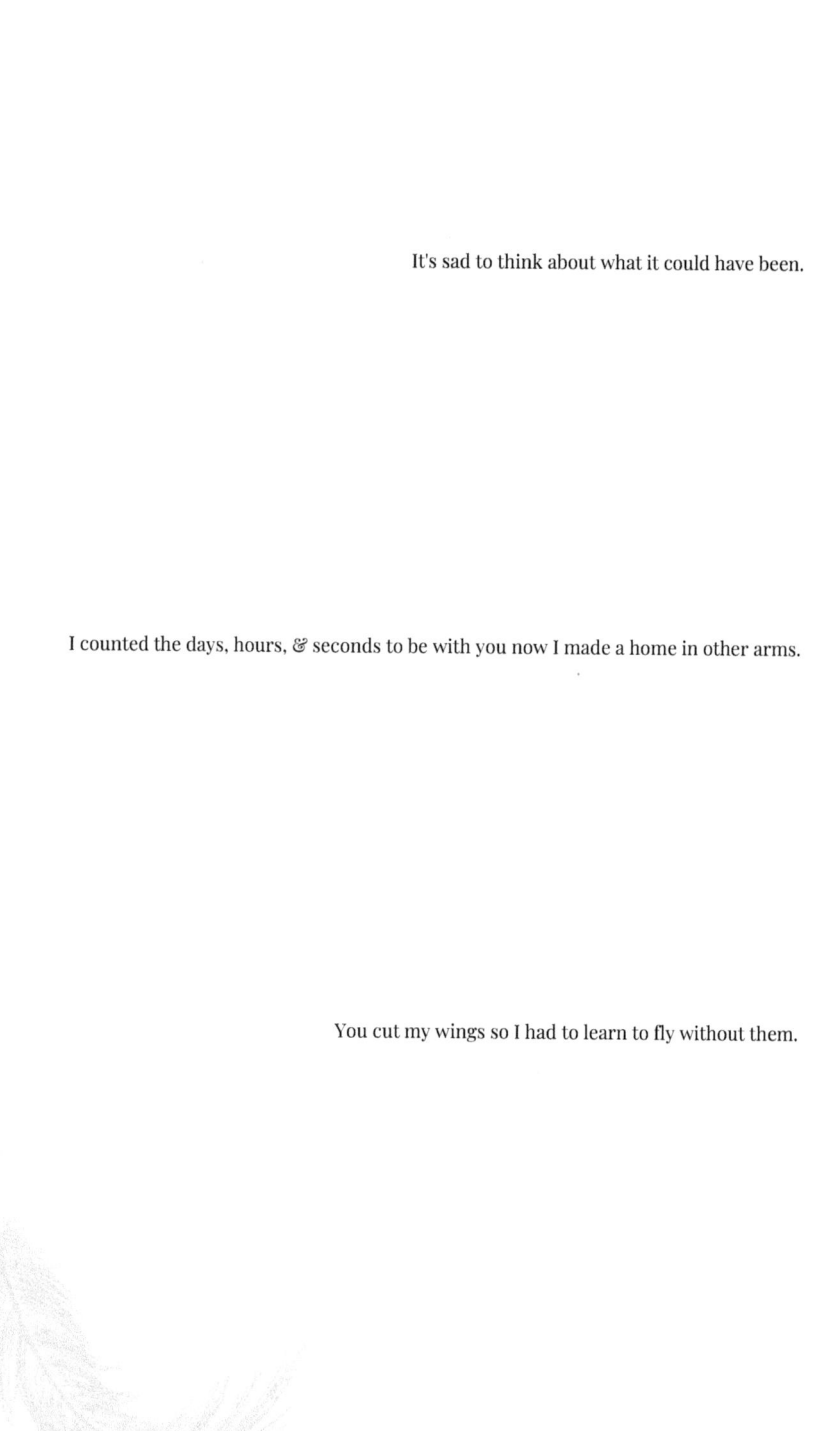

The name rolls off the tongue like poison. Forbidden fruit. A simple touch burns. Safe distance, must keep. The addiction runs deep.

What is she holding on to? More heartbreak, more lies, more unfaithfulness. Sometimes holding on hurts more than letting go.

I look at her and remember she's had you too. As my blood begins to boil. She think she's won the battle. But it's me you still want. That makes her cringe. You can never be me.

Did you think of me? The effect, the broken heart, the mistrust.
Was it worth it? The temporary pleasure.
Did you regret? The feeling of guilt and shame.
Did you think I would never find out? Reoccurring occasion.
Did you not love me? You don't break those you love.
And then I sat, numb, unable to move, for number of hours.
Thinking........
Was it me?
Were they better?
Am I not worth it?
I am living a lie.
Is she prettier?
Did she love him?
Why?
I gave you my all.
Why wasn't that enough?
I would have stayed.
But you didn't care.
The pain was too much.
I walked away......

Betrayal

I'll never let anyone in like you made yourself in. From outside in you knew me. Dreams, fears, secrets, you figured them all out. Like it was your purpose to make me transparent to you. The words came out my mouth but you read in between the lines. The lies, you knew even before they were told. My thoughts were stolen just from a look in my eyes. As the next step was planned to be taken you were calculating. You said you liked that I kept you on your toes but I was just dodging the feelings, trying to keep them as my own.

The winter is colder. The nights are longer. Spring is short. Days are slow. Music has no sound. Lyrics has no meaning. Flowers don't blossom. The picture is gray. Life with depression is so unbalanced.

Circumstances bring certain choices
From the choices comes consequences
Consequences are what you are living now
Everyone has different circumstances
Therefore everyone has difference choices
Everyone is living in their own consequence

My Anxiety

Palms sweaty

Chest tight

Fidgeting

Can't keep still

Mind racing

Thoughts

Uncontrollable thoughts

Overwhelmed

Pacing

Back & forth, back & forth

Increasing breaths

Deep breaths

Doesn't help

Whispering to yourself

Be calm

Stay still

Body not listening

No control

Drowning

Exhaustion

Oh, the exhaustion

Hurt People Hurt People

When you met her she was just a friend. You got to know her and enjoyed her company. Asked her to be your girl but had no intention of loving her, no intentions on treating her right. She fell head over heels just like you knew she would. You played the sickest games and she couldn't let go. Hurt after hurt, betrayal after betrayal, she stayed. She thought this was love but abuse isn't love. She didn't have a clue. It was the final straw and she was done. Then you realized you really did love her but it was too late. She moved on. But you turned her into a monster. She knew no love. She knew no loyalty, all she knew was hurt. Her heart cold. She turned around and did the same thing you did to the next. He ended doing time for a crime he didn't commit. He paid the price for your lies. When all he wanted to do was love. And this is why they say hurt people hurt people.

It doesn't care if you're rich or poor.

It doesn't care if you're young or old.

It doesn't care if you're male or female.

It doesn't care if you're married or single.

It doesn't care if you're an entrepreneur or have a nine to five.

It doesn't care if you laugh and smile or cry and pout all-day.

It doesn't care if you have all the high-end cars or riding your bike.

When depression strikes it doesn't matter what you have, it strikes.

You can't see it but you feel it.

You can't show it but it's there.

Consuming,

Lying.

It was like we played this nasty game of who could hurt who more. I'm sure you won because I've never felt this way before.

I can admit I'm not good with changes. It takes a while for me to let go. I like to keep things how they are and when they are good and it changes, it messes me up the most. I reminisce on those beautiful memories, wishing I could relive them. Wishing they'd never end. Trying to recreate them, it doesn't happen the same way. Changes are not good for me. Why can't it stay how it is, or how it was, when it was good?

The heart stayed beating for you. No matter how hard she tried to unlove you, the heart kept beating your name.
You can get so lost in this world.
Lost in others,
lost in materialism,
lost in the media,
lost in the unreal,
lost in your own damn mind.
Look in the mirror and not even recognize yourself.
Who am I?
How did I get where I am?
Are you living or just moving through the motions?
Draw a map and never lose yourself again.

How can I be jealous over what isn't mine? You made me feel like yours after all this time.

We just all want to be okay, but we're not. We're all broken.

Your memory is painful but somehow, it's my favorite pain.

If you take away your love, you take away my sanity.

In my next life I'll search for you, I promise.

You get so wrapped up in your thoughts that suddenly you want to cry and not know why.

I told you I would search for you in our next lifetime and you responded, if it didn't happen in this one, it wasn't meant to be.

And when we kissed this time around, it was different because my lips belonged to someone else.

Look me in the eyes and tell me you don't love me. Look me in the eyes and tell me you don't crave me. Look me in the eyes and tell me I don't burn deep through your veins. Look me in the eyes and tell me that our connection isn't true. Tell me, because that's just the saddest lie.

He was good until he met me.
I tested everything and over and over again he fell.
I enjoyed the power.
Never tasted anything like it.
Sweet and sour.
I knew it was wrong but I couldn't stop.
Always dominated never dominate....until now. Tasted too good.

Don't want to fall in love again

Don't want to give a heart that's been lied to, beaten, and damage

Don't want to fall to get lied, beaten, and damaged again

Don't want to fall in love, this heart is fragile

Love is a lie!

I wasn't able to love you like you deserved. I hope you found someone who can. Someone to appreciate your kisses like I didn't, someone to embrace your presences like I should have, someone to return the smiles instead of lies. You deserve to be loved like you love.

There is ink splattered all over the floor, from your broken heart. I told you to pick up the pieces and walk out. The only mess I need is my own, I cannot carry your burden anymore.

My innocence was murdered by your lies.
My thoughts have never been the same since the introduction into your wicked world.
Things that aren't good don't seem bad.
Where is the innocent girl who loved with all her heart and cared genuinely about others feelings?
I miss her.

If you sit and try to listen to my thoughts, you'll get lost in a never-ending maze. Feels like a game. What you put in isn't always what you get out. Many words are lost in translation. It's been tried to put them in the order the thoughts are supposed to be, but who's right? I'm never right. I'm always wrong, remember. It's what you always repeated. Over and over. Who can I blame for these dark secrets? The black thoughts? The gray feelings? I don't want to blame myself. I'm messed up as it is. Can I blame the voices? They wake up when they want to. Only when convenient for you. No, it's okay. Life is just a game. Are you winning?

How selfish of me to ask if we could stay friends after our adventure but I wanted you in my life, even if it's just friends.

She told me to make a choice. Looks like you're making it for me. This time it isn't the chapter that's ending, it's the book.

Why did you make me apologize for being me? Instead of being compassionate and try to understand, you made me feel like I was the problem. That's the thing with manipulation, you don't realize its being done until years later.

How come you couldn't love me?
Was it me?
Was it something I did?
Something I said?
How come you couldn't love me?
Should I have done more?
Was I not enough?
How come you couldn't love me?
I could change my hair for you.
I could change my clothes for you.
I could change the way I walk, maybe the way I talk?
How come you couldn't love me?
Everything you asked for I did.
Everything you wanted I give.
How come you couldn't love me?

You were so sweet with all the right words to say. You felt heaven sent or was it all in my head? Sadness when you had to leave. Butterflies and warm tingling feelings at the mention of your name, or was it all in my head? The craving for love was so intense that the confusion for lust remain. We were picture perfect, all smiles, but it was all in my head.

Nowadays we are so afraid of committing that we love from a distance. Won't be together but act like we are together and we can't dare see each other with someone else.

You had a void that needed to be filled. I wasn't going to be the one to fill it. I had built up anger that needed to be unleashed. And I released it on the wrong person. We were great but the timing was off. What you needed I couldn't offer, can't pour from an empty cup. What I needed was to cope and I found sex. We were a beautiful disaster.

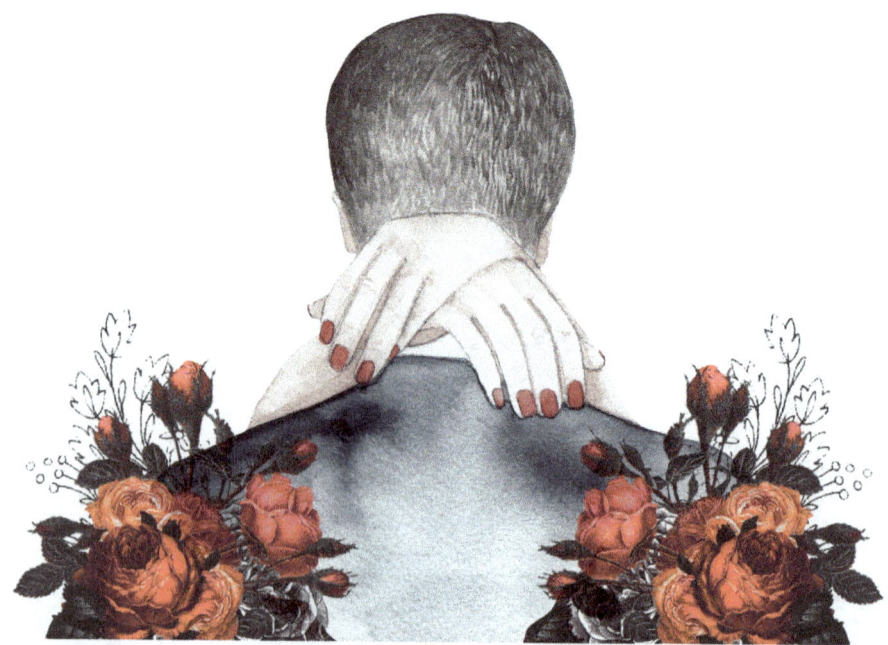

I need you to understand that in my mind nothing is sane. Complete chaos is what roars through the tongue and nothing more. I don't get me; you won't get me. Don't even try.

Was my heart wrong in loving you? Was my heart wrong in forgiving you so much? Was my heart wrong in believing in you? You left it in pieces - each time. Although, it kept choosing you, it broke, until it couldn't break anymore. Now it's scattered all over the floor, waiting for someone to pick it up and make it whole again. It should be me, but I'm too weak. Not enough energy to move. Have you ever tired moving with a broken heart? It's exhausting. Have you ever tried breathing with a broken heart, it's a sharp pain since there's no air. My energy is spent on the simple gestures and minimal efforts that's barely keeping me alive. My heart is gone and so is my life, slowly, fading away.

Let's pretend we are meant to be. Let's pretend the timing was right. Let's pretend you are mine and I am yours. Let's pretend our souls connected at a deeper level. Let's pretend our kisses were magical. Let's pretend our love making sparked fireworks. Let's pretend we are together, even if it's only for a second.

He was a forbidden fruit she wanted to bite. Although she knew it would kill her slowly inside. No cares given, she bit and bit. Addicted to the adrenaline he brought. Addicted to the high she got. She slowly lost herself in him and him in her.

This cannot be real, this cannot be right. All the yelling, screaming, and fighting - this cannot be life. This cannot be how you want to live. I miss my peace. I miss my harmony. Are you willing to work with me, baby? Let's get back to love baby. Like two wild teenagers whose hormones are crazy.

Could the rain wash the insecurities? Temporary. The mirror reflects the truth.

Her heart was so soft for him. He found it easy to walk all over it. Took advantage of a good heart should be the ultimate crime. But the good heart can only take so much. Until it's time to mend on its own.

Watching you cry & beg for me made me feel a little sorry, not too much. How can you hurt someone you love? Now, you feel what I've been feeling for years. It took you seeing me with someone else, finally moved on, to realize what you had, when I was always there for you. I bet you never thought you'd see the day that I moved on. But guess what, I did & I'm glad I did. Cry, cry all the tears I cried for you, it's your turn. Funny how the tables have turned.

If you felt what I felt, you would have fought to stay together. Because from what I felt I would have never let go. Not in a million years.

The last page is always the hardest to turn

Because it's the end of the story

What if you're not ready to close the book

But you're unable to write a different ending.

HEALING

Diving into the unknown is terrifying, but sometimes from the unknown is where we most grow. Embrace the unknown

I've fought battles in this life that weren't my own. Because my love surpassed it all.
Now, it's time to love myself just as much or a little more.

The hands of time don't go back. Do the same and move on. This is not a revolving door. Once its closed, it's done.

I gave so much there's nothing left. Now, I'm left searching for the missing pieces. Slowing developing myself again.

It's hard loving the broken pieces, but you've been doing just fine. Molding me back to whole.

She's an immediate catch to the eye. Fierce.

By the battles won she's become a fierce warrior.

There is something mysterious about her. For when she talks, she leaves you lingering for more.

Unlike Adele, I don't want someone like you. I do wish you the best and best of luck to the next girl. I hope you treat her better.

Listen to the rain drops, the love song they create as they fall on your window. Feel the wind as the cold breakthrough. Reach the clouds as they become available to play.

You've kissed away the pain. You've wiped away the fears. You've gently brought me back to confidence.

The cold reminds me of your absence warmth. The broken dreams have become the reality. The norm I used to know is no longer the norm. Time to adjust.

Somedays I'll be happy and smiling from ear to ear for no reason. Other days I'll be quiet and keep to myself. Somedays I'll be talkative and can keep a conversation going. Other days I'll be down and don't know why. Those are the days I'll need your hugs a little tighter and your love a little stronger. Thank you.

Years of trauma takes a toll on the mind and body. Recovering takes just as long as the trauma, if not longer. Nightmares come - bad memories will appear but trust the process. Healing is coming soon.

You ever look at an old picture of yourself and remember the pain you were feeling? I no longer want to look back at pain, I want to look at joy and peace.

Sometimes I believe you, sometimes I don't. Please be patient as my trust builds, after being lied to so many times before.
- *Trauma*

Working on overcoming the hurt with love of oneself. Realizing ones worth - realizing ones value you become unstoppable. Never again give the power to someone else to make you feel like you're not good enough. They aren't good enough for you. Love yourself first! Fill your cup! Be yourself.

My tears weren't motive enough for you to stop the pain. The realization of the mistreatment took far too long. This is your loss. And with this one I'll stand strong.

Don't forget to be free.

It will all fall back together after you let go; was the hardest lesson to learn.

I want to see me through your eyes.

We all have our journey; we all have our path. Just as unique as we are.

My time may not be your time, your time may not be my time. Although we all have the same time, don't compare my time to your time.

I don't think you've ever realized how your choices effect those around you. Those who care about you. You hurt them. You were toxic, to yourself, to them and now we are all left with a scar deep in our soul. Years of damage take years to recover. I'm working on it.

Listen closely to the silence, that's when she speaks the loudest. Look closely at the blank stare that's when she shows the emotion. She will demonstrate what she needs, you just have to pay attention.

Every day she wakes up, dresses up, and pretends to be a fearless, confident, resilient woman. But then comes home, takes off that mask and goes to sleep with a lonely heart and her monsters.

The healing process is a journey. Be patient. Some days are clear, some days are foggy but it's part of healing the broken road. Just as it took time to break you down it takes time to build you back up. Be kind to yourself

As days go by, I'll think of you less and less. Soon you'll become a distance memory sitting in the back with dust like forgotten old books.

Holding on to you was like walking with bricks on both my legs. I needed to let go in order to move forward

Could it be that I love the pain? Could it be that I'm so used to being hurt that that has become my new norm. All I know is hurt. I want to know healing, I want to know forgetting, I want to know calmness, no more anxiety, no more depression, no more mood swings. I want peace.

Embrace your flaws, they are what makes you most beautiful. Embrace your imperfections, they are what makes you most perfect. Embrace your scars, they are what makes you most brave. Embrace your battles, they are what makes you a warrior.

Search deep within yourself the courage to carry the burden of everyday life can get overwhelming sometimes it's hard to see the light at the end of the tunnel or even when the sun will shine. The weight is heavy, peace will soon take over, and when it does, it will be marvelous.

Do not doubt yourself, release that fear from your mind. It is a trap.

It's a daily struggle to remind yourself how great you really are. Think back of everything you've overcome and you're still here. You're a rockstar

If it seems like the rain never hurts, it does. If it seems like sun never shines, it does. If it seems like the clouds are never white, they are. Look beyond the horizon. Feel beyond the pain. Run past the finish line. Never mind the shame. Learn from the discomfort and grow within the vision, sometimes the best things are without reason.

Her tears turned into fire, passionately burning for victory. No more pain, change the narrative. You're a survivor, never the same.

Soon it will all be a distant memory

Fading away

Keep going

Writing doesn't take the pain away; it lets me express it.

Poetry speaks what the mouth can't say. Poetry shows what the heart feels. Poetry finds what's hidden inside. Poetry helps heal the wounds. Poetry reveals the soul.

So many things and occasions that I thought I wouldn't make it, but yet here I stand.

Lies

For years I fed myself lies

Accusations - assumptions - never facts

I slowly destroyed myself

Pretending

Wanting to be something I wasn't

Trying to please - acceptance

Wanting to be wanted

Trying to fulfill a void

A hole so deep

Each day I dug deeper unloving myself.

Can't look in the mirror - reflects my true self

Can't bear to look at her.

The pain of losing you is more than I thought I could ever bare. But here I am, still breathing, still feeling, still beating.

It's time to take care of yourself after spending many years taking care of others. Daily reminder, you cannot fill from an empty cup. Sometimes you have to water yourself and watch yourself blossom.

She came

She poured love

She dried up

She left

There came a point where I lost myself. I lost myself within you. I lost myself trying to please you. I lost myself giving you the world on a silver platter. I was so consumed by you I placed your happiness above my own. I lived for you, day and night, everything was you. I could only see you, hear you, taste you, breath you. There was no one else but you. I vow to never lose myself again.

You can hide the pain behind the smile, but you cannot hide the pain behind the words.

I miss you but that doesn't mean I want you back. Because I can miss you and not want you back.

For so long I had to pretend to be happy, it became second nature - while it burned inside. While I screamed deeply and painfully.

The biggest battles I fight are always with myself.

When you've been hurt the same way again the scars from old wounds start to bleed again.

There is beauty in pain. Look closer, you are a diamond in the making.

One day you'll realize my love was pure and unconditional. I never had bad intentions. You'll realize I just wanted to be loved how I loved you but by then your time will be up.

I loved you more than I loved myself and that cannot happen again.

I was angry
So angry
All the time
Everything triggered me
The smallest thing would turn into a huge argument
It was exhausting
Seemed like people had to walk on eggshells around me
Nothing would make me happy
No one can possibly live okay being so angry
The anger was so consuming
Wasted energy

Speak love to yourself.
Speak life unto yourself.
Be gentle with yourself.
And learn to forgive yourself.
-part of healing

You could say the thoughts of you scare me.
Why do you still visit me in my dreams?
I don't belong to you.
You ruled over me for years.
My mind is mine and my body is mine.
Your darkness cannot overshadow me anymore - you have no power against me.
Are you lonely?
That's how you had me, isolated even in a room full of people.
Alone in my mind.
You made me do things I didn't approve of.
You made me say things I didn't agree to.
You made me think things I didn't believe.
You had me convinced I wasn't worthy, loved, or valued.
I broke free of your power.
I broke the chains and ran away.

-depression

The wounds are deep but the scars are hollow. The scars are the reflection of the intangible pain. The wounds and scars tell the story. Story of triumph.

What I do - don't do, say or don't say. What I withhold or choose to share has to do nothing to do with you and everything to do with me. My healing is my responsibility because my trauma wasn't.

Heels strapped & with red lipstick on, she can conquer the world.

Loneliness has been my biggest fear. Because I've witness what it does to us.
Depression, crying, drives you to drink, desperation, and no happiness near sight.
The fear triggered many choices and actions.
Some not so great.
I couldn't be alone with myself.
The thoughts that would creep scared me.
Loneliness is a monster; I couldn't defeat on my own.

The thoughts are scattered, place them together and they could tell a story. Of love, of triumph, or heartbreak. You decide.

You had me constantly comparing myself to other females. Trying to find what they had that I didn't have to make you want them instead of me. Now you can't have me, but you don't want them. I no longer need validation; I am me and I am enough.

She screamed in the dark no one heard she put a fight. She cried to sleep night after night. She thought love would shed the light, to a world she never knew. She failed herself - she lost herself. In circles there she goes - no destination nowhere to go. This is her last chance to make it right. Before she gives up, this is her last fight.

Unfortunately. Many will not achieve the art of self-love. Still seeking validation from others. Danger lies in that due to not everyone loves themselves. See the curse? How can you find love in someone who doesn't love themselves? It's nonexistent. Seek within yourself acceptance in who you are. Say I am enough, enough times until you believe it.

In the darkest days with the darkest thoughts a force bigger than anything pulled me through the waters. The thoughts consumed me, overwhelming told me to let go, nothing was worth it, but the force wouldn't let go. The force wouldn't give up, the force was the life savior.

I thought the dreams about the trauma
were done.
But you showed up last night.
It was the same thing over again.
The lying, the sneaking, the betrayal.
I thought I moved passed this.
I thought this was over.
But yet there are the nightmares haunting me.
Reminding me of my past.
How when I felt I wasn't good enough.
Of when I felt I wasn't woman enough.
The time when the hurt cut so deep.
Physically felt like a knife was stabbed in my chest.
My stomach was put into a knot.
And a lump in my throat would not go down.
So many years of trauma. A few months couldn't undo all the damage.
I guess back to work on myself I go.
Unveiling all the past hurt and wounds.

How can you see where you're going if your eyes are always looking down? Look up my child, be proud of who you are.

Fears reveal insecurities the battles within ourselves who we want to be, who we should be, and who we are. Unravel the soul peeling the layers one by one

It was painful to walk away. I couldn't think. I couldn't breathe. I wouldn't sleep. Why does love hurt so much? No, my darling. That wasn't love, love doesn't hurt. The risk of handing over your bare heart to someone and having them crush it little by little into pieces hurts. But that's not love. The desire to have them water you and help you grow but instead they only feed their ego with your presence and energy, hurts. But that's not love. Giving your all to someone and receiving nothing in return is draining leaving you dry, hurts, but that's not love! Love is not hard. Love doesn't hurt. Love comes easily, for two compatible hearts.

The same broken record continues to play. The lyrics remain the same, the chorus, the bridge. You know this song all too well. Take it off repeat, the ending is the same. Time for a new dance.

Not even all the damage made to her soul could dim her light.

I don't want to be the me I was before you, she was fragile. Now I'm stronger and love harder.

To fall easily is a weakness because not everyone is willing to catch you. Many are good at disguise.

Her soul is gentle, she's been broken but she doesn't let it define her. She's not just surviving, she's thriving.

The pain of losing you hurt most. I had so many hopes for you, dreams, and plans. Before you came I had names. I had announcements planned. I had pretty pictures in my head for your arrival. Although the time was extremely short with you inside, I had so much joy in my heart. Knowing you were conceived with so much love and happiness.
I love you forever. Baby De La Cruz ❤

MOTHER

You gave me saggy boobs and leaks of golden liquid. You gave me a bigger stomach and stripes to go with it. You gave me wider hips and more hair. You gave me exhaustion and change of appetite. But overall, you gave me life.

As the witness of the attempted murder of your own life, is there things we can unsee?

The news of your departure was something inexpressible. As my brain processed you were gone the empty feeling became the new norm. You took a part of me with you. I'll never feel whole again.

I will speak life onto my daughter, I will build her up, not tear her down. I will build her skin tough for when the world tries to break her, she will know she's stronger than anything else. Positive influence, she will know others are not competition. She will focus on her own and help others along the way. I will speak life into my daughter.

You asked for help, and I ran immediately. I dropped everything; I stopped my life for you. But you didn't want any help. You drained me out. Exhaustion didn't even come close. I gave my all for nothing because the notice wasn't even there. Last words spoken were hurtful, painful. Although you didn't know, I forgave you. And I always loved you and I'll always love you. With your monsters and all.

No one else has authority over my body. I'm the one bearing the pain. I'm the one who will carry the child. I'm the one who decides when and where. Respect my body. Respect my choice.

You choose to not be a parent and it was probably the best choice you made. Because you couldn't parent. But there were consequences with that choice. Having your child try to fill that void with others. Others that weren't meant to fill it.

A child that lacks security develops anxiety. Needing love and nourishment from their mom but the mom doesn't know how to provide builds an insecure adult. The person who is supposed to protect is the one who places the child in danger. Recovery is a long road to undo the damage.

There was a dent in my heart long before you came and made your wedge. I just didn't know. It was made by a lady. Who would have been my first protector. She introduced me to anxiety. To the feeling of being unsafe. I can't blame her, and I can't hate her. There are people my heart just cannot hate.

I needed to feel secured, and you could never provide that sense of security.

The person who was supposed to make me feel safe, was the one causing me anxiety.

I want to give her the security I didn't have. The comfort I missed and the safe heaven I never had.

I'm proud of the mother I am and the child she is.

The words that your offspring is well behaved and sweet is music to a mother's ear. Washes a feeling of relief over you. It's worth it, she listens, you think. You smile, squeeze her tight and kiss her! Their behavior says more about your parenting than clothes ever will. Nor Ralph Lauren, Gucci, Michael Kor will ever show or tell what a decent human someone is. Actions and kind words. Helpfulness, respect, obedience says more.

R
A
I
N
B
O
W

You've left me wordless because what I feel I cannot explain.

If my lips say, "I love you", believe them, those words aren't for everyone.

You've made an imprint in my heart and forever it will stay.

You've made your mark within me, I may wonder, but my heart and mind is always with you.

To stop thinking about you, is to stop breathing.

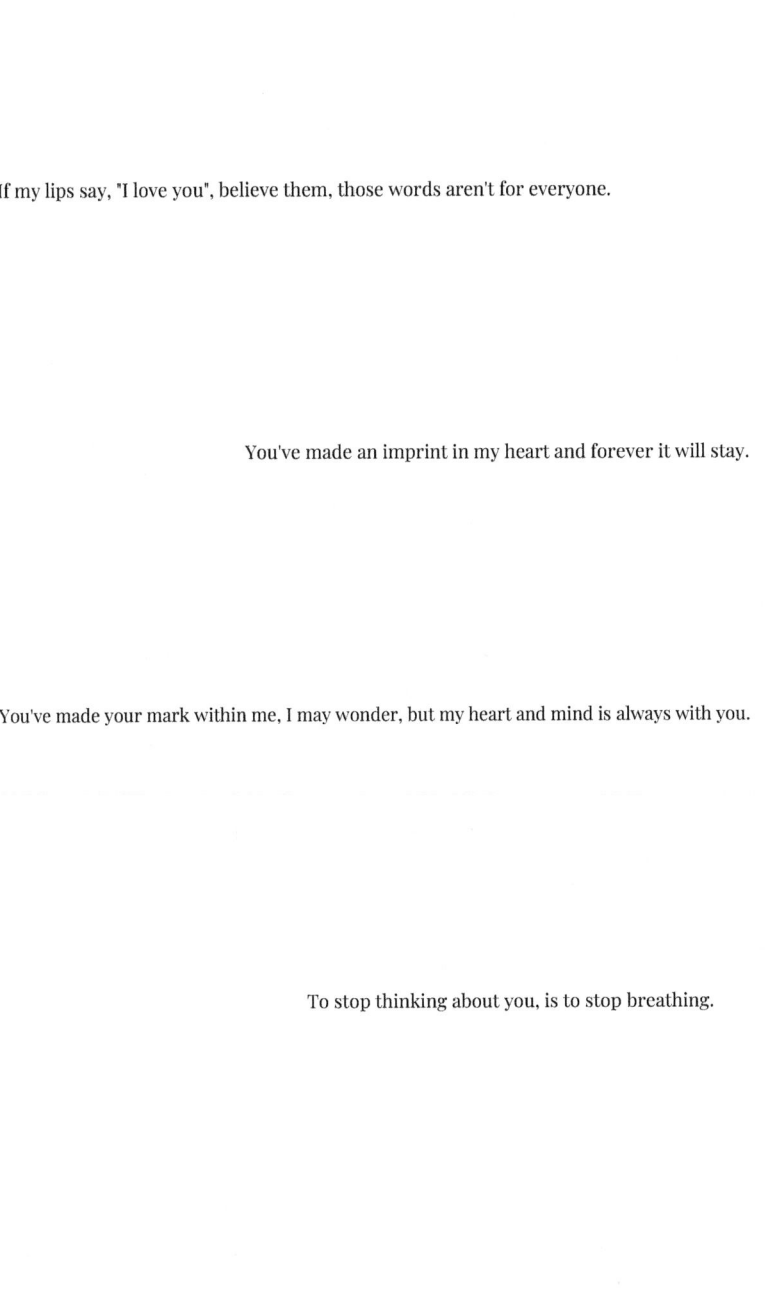

The dreams spoke to me, told me that you've been seeking me. I told them to make sure my name never rolls off your tongue, while my heart pounding, wanting to seek you too.

To be loved correctly, in your love language, fills you up. Provides comfort, ease. A smile for no reason, a new glow.

He wants to wipe your tears and make sure you never cry again.

Why do you love me he asked

I don't know she whispered

That's how I know you really love me

He replied, as he leaned to kiss her forehead

There's a connection that we have. It's not anything I have felt with anyone else. Can't quite put my finger on it. But I love it.

I enjoy making you laugh; it's pleasing to know I'm the reason behind your smile

Today I celebrate you. Because of you, your love, and your patience, I've been able to blossom again. I love you.

-Anniversary

Don't close the door on love, it will come knocking when you least expect it. Make you forget you were ever hurt or broken.

I was under the impression in order to find love I would have to change so much about me, until I met someone who loves me for me and doesn't want to change a thing.

Because of you love songs make sense. Because of you the smiles come for no reason. Because of you fears have flown away. Because of you love returned. Because of you there is freedom.

There is a connection between you and I that words cannot express. There is a connection between you and I that it's not commonly seen. There is a connection between you and I that is pure bliss when we become one. There is a connection between you and I that I never want to lose. There's a connection between you and I that want to grow deeper. There's a connection between you and I that I'll cherish forever.

Of all the words there are 3 that when placed together have the most meaning but have been repeated and said with emptiness and lies behind it, that it's hard to believe when told now.

- I love you

They say when it rains it pours but as long as you're by my side we can dance in the rain together.

There's a sparkle in your eyes when you look at me that sets my soul on fire.

Let me explore your mind. I want to discover hidden treasures. Let me take an adventure within you. I want my findings to expose a whole new world.

Lay your head on my chest boy, I'll provide support and comfort. Make you forget you were ever hurt before.

Take my hand, let's get lost in the galaxy. Create our own world. Nothing else matters, as long as I'm with you.

The light is green, but I refuse to move without you as my passenger.

Thinking of the way you handle me, caress me, gently touch me, makes my hairs stand up. Kiss me gently but passionately.

Sooner or later the broken pieces will fit perfectly together projecting a beautiful picture of you
and I.

As we lay at night remembering our actions that has brought us into today. I hope none you regret and it's all you've ever wanted. To lay down beside me nightly and wake up with me daily.

You are my favorite poem to write.

I may not know what tomorrow brings, but I know that I trust you. The present is what matters to me because you're in it. If for some reason you decide to walk away, I know I gave all my love to you. I don't want to know what it feels like to lose you. I may not know what the future holds, all I know is that I love you.

I wanted to keep you as my little secret as long as I could, people ruin good things as fast as they can.

Any news, good or bad, you're the first person to know. Any situation I come across, you're the first person to know. Any changes that occur, you're the first person to know. I run to you because you are my home.

As we laid, back to chest, it felt unreal. I kissed your back, felt your arm and ask, "is this real?"

The moon is waiting for us to open the door of our hearts, let the light shine bright within.

Oh, how I missed the butterflies of a new love. The innocent child-like jitters. The smirk after seeing their name light up your phone. Knowing you're thinking of them while they think of you. The anticipation of when you'll see them next. Butterflies, you've been missed.

You committed the perfect crime, stole my heart before I knew it was stolen. All you've done is take care of it, mend it back together, fix the broken pieces. Please don't repair it to break it again.

I prayed for a love like this. Now, that I have a love like this, I pray for everyone to find a love like this.

Your poetry is beautiful. The way your words flow making no sense and at the same time making perfect sense. How you must read between the lines but read from right to left. Your poetry is beautiful, keep them wondering; keep them guessing.

Love me softly, love me gently, love me deeply, love me passionately. Love me like no other.

Stimulate my mind, make love to my soul.

And this I know to be true. I can definitely do life with you.

The music died in his soul when love went away. No more lyrics. No more rhyme. No more bridges. No more harmony. Learning to sing again. He found his voice again. The melody returned bringing music back to his soul. A new love began. The love of his own voice.

Baby, hold me tight through the night. It's cold outside and I need that skin to skin. I need to know you'll be there. Cover me with your presence.

Let me be good to you. Let me water you & help you grow. Let me cater to you. Let me care for you & love you.

The road to recovery is a bumpy ride. I know I'll be able to continue with you by my side. I'll drive and you be my passenger. No one else I would share this road with.

Can you interpret my dreams? You always seem to appear in them. Can you interpret my silence? You always seem to fill it. Can you interpret my thoughts? You always seem to pop up. Can you interpret my heart? You seem to have stolen it.

The paint brush of life has the colors of the wind. Beauty is the color you paint it.

Who knew that after the heartbreak I would be able to trust again? Who knew that after the tears I would be able to smile again? Who knew that after all the damage I would be able to love again? Who knew? You knew.

Tell me which story is your favorite? It drips from your mouth like gold. Tell me your thoughts, don't be afraid mine are darker. The mind wonders and goes into a black hole, sucks you in won't release until you go numb. The water of sorrow is what wakes you, you cannot escape your mind. Pour out to me. Transfer the demons, I'll battle them with you. Let me in. I live in the darkness but at least we will be together.

Love knows no pain if there is pain it isn't love. Love knows no restrictions if there is no freedom it isn't love. Love knows no boundaries because its unconditional if there's conditions it isn't love. Love knows no suffering, no betrayal, no lies. Love always prevails.

My inspiration comes full force at night. As I sit and think about you, such a blessing. How you protect me. Such a force. How you love me, such gentleness. How you care for me, such grace. But most importantly, how patient you are with me. My love, what did I do to deserve such perfect love?

Writing a poem a day keeps me sane.

I could tell the world about how great your love is. But I know they will get tired of me only talking about you. I just never experience something so real, so raw, so natural, so amazing ever. A person who chooses me every day. Wakes up and tries to make my day better. Cares so much and will insistently know when something is off because he pays attention. To make sure I'm okay is a daily thing. And I want to give you all that and more. I know sometimes I fail. There are days that it's all about me and days that it's all about you. There are days that it's all about us. But no matter what, my love for you grows deeper every day. Let's continue to nourish our love. Let's continue to water it and make it grow. Grow naturally, no pressure, effortlessly. You are all I ever needed. You are all I ever wanted. You are all I was made believe didn't existed. You are all for me and I for you. I love how you love me!